S0-ARL-865

Third Print 1999

Published by:

INTERNATIONAL EVANGELICAL RESOURCE CENTRE
P. O. Box 11057
Dorpspruit, 32056, South Africa

AGAINST THE TIDES IN THE MIDDLE EAST

A TRUE STORY ABOUT

MUSTAFA
FORMER TEACHER OF ISLAMIC HISTORY
AT AL AZHAR UNIVERSITY, CAIRO, EGYPT

Dedication 1

To the oppressed people of the world, who are prisoners of injustice, who have lost their way, who are searching for salvation, justice, mercy and life.

To these people I dedicate my own trials and experiences so that they may be encouraged with a candle to light the way.

Dedication 2

To my beloved and faithful friend Salah Mahmoud

I received the news of your arrest because of your preaching about Jesus Christ.

They tried hard to make you abandon your faith in Jesus Christ, but they failed. Then they killed you by electric shock and sent your body to your family. Your father refused to accept it because you were no longer the son that he knew.

Who ever thought that you will die as a martyr for the sake of the name of Jesus Christ, the name against which you fought and inflicted harm to those who believed in it. How many pharmacies and stores owned by Christians have you burnt? How many Christians have you killed? Who ever thought that a miracle will happen in your heart, that you would go through this radical change? It was all possible because of the Lord Jesus Christ who saved you and gave you eternal life.

I love you, friend of my childhood. My heart weeps inside me for your departure. My only comfort is that you are now in heaven with Him whom you have loved and sacrificed your life for, the Lord Jesus Christ.

Many write their life story with ink and I am one of them. But few are those who write it with their own blood, and you are one of them. You were my student in the Christian faith, today the student surpassed his teacher.

Where am I from you, martyr? Where am I from you, friend?

- Mustafa

CHAPTER 1

'Where is that traitor of a son', my father shouted beside himself with rage. *'What will people say- what will I say to Allah on the day of judgement - my son is a traitor to ISLAM!'*

I was hiding inside my sister's house hearing every word my father was saying. I had fled there only minutes before in a desperate attempt to save my life. Then, for the first time I realised that I would never be able to return home or ever again live in my own country - Egypt. Every man's hand yearned to be against me. I was about to become a refugee. My whole life had changed in less than a day. That very morning, I boldly wore a cross around my neck. My father saw the cross...

'What's this?' He cried. I told him it was a cross.
'What!' He cried.
'This is a cross and I am a Christian!' I said.

At once he fainted and fell to the floor. My brothers rushed to help him up. When he regained his senses, he immediately grabbed a small handgun and fired five bullets at me. None of them hit me. As my father attempted to kill me I ran out of the house and fled to my sister's house, with my father in hot pursuit. Banging on the door, yelling hysterically, my father demanded that my sister open the door...

1. MY BIRTH AND CHILDHOOD

I was born on December 30, 1957, to Muslim parents in upper Egypt, the region known as Al Saeed. My parents and my extended family were devout Muslims. My father owned a clothing factory as well as a few plots of land. My mother was a housewife. I had six brothers and a sister. My brothers all completed their studies at Egyptian universities, but my sister was not at all educated - neither at school nor university. This was not unusual - denying girls an education was customary not only in upper Egypt, but also throughout the Muslim world.

When I began to mature and observe the world around me, I found myself to be in the hands of my uncle who had graduated with a master's degree from the esteemed Al Azhar university in Cairo. My uncle was a master of the Qur'an and his task was to make me memorise the entire Qur'an, but without any tangible understanding of it's meaning... I was five years old at the time.

One day when I was sitting beside my uncle reciting the Qur'an, a relative said to my uncle: *'Sheikh Mohammed, our nephew Mustafa, from his infancy, drank the milk from the breast of Omm William, the wife of your neighbour, Hanna Botros the Christian.'*
'Yes I know,' my uncle replied, *'does it bother you?'*
'I swear on Allah,' the man answered, *'my Sheikh Mowlana, I am afraid, for this boy might convert to Christianity when he is older.'*
My uncle replied with: *'Don't be afraid, I taught him the Qur'an from infancy, as you can see. By next year I will enrol him at Al Azhar school where the Qur'an will protect him. So there's no need for us to worry.'*

2. THE CHRISTIAN WOMAN

If the Muslims are afraid of Christian women breast-feeding their children, why do they permit it? My parents told me that when I was young, I had a serious illness. I refused to drink the milk from my mother's breast. My mother tried everything to make me drink from her, but every time, to her dismay, I refused. My mother brought many Muslim women, among them neighbours and relatives who attempted to feed me. But I refused them and became physically weaker and weaker. I was just a breath away from death, and my mother would place me on her lap and weep. Each attempt to feed me was futile. I obstinately refused to drink from any Muslim woman. Then one day, our Christian neighbour, Omm William, came to enquire about me. Hearing how ill I was, Omm William said: *'My*

son William was born on the same day as your son Mustafa. I still have plenty of milk for both of them. Here, give me Mustafa, perhaps he will accept my milk.'
My mother placed me on Omm William's lap. Before Omm William gave me her breast she whispered: *'In the Name of Christ'*
At this point I screamed violently. My mother, upon witnessing this, began to tremble. She rebuked Omm William harshly for saying it: *'What blasphemy! What apostasy!'* But after she had said these words, my mother's tongue froze. She sat in disbelief as she watched my mouth go to Omm William's breast. I fed from her until I was satisfied, then in complete contentment I fell asleep on Omm William's lap.

Relieved, my mother kissed Omm William all over her face. When my father arrived my mother explained the situation to him. My father decided that Omm William was to feed me every day.

This act could have led to the acceptance of Christ by my staunch Muslim family but their dedication to Islam blinded them.

3. ENTRANCE INTO AL AZHAR[1] MEMORISING THE QUR'AN

My uncle enrolled me in Al Azhar school at the age of six. My teacher in the first year of school was the Sheikh Ibrahim, a tall, forbidding, one eyed man with a harsh voice and a stick was a permanent fixture in his hand. It was this man who taught us the

---

[1] Al Azhar
Oldest and largest Islamic university in the world situated in Cairo with 100 000 pupils from Egypt and other countries.
Al Azhar is a very large educational institution, finances come from many different sources and many countries and Islamic banks contribute to the one billion dollars received every year.
Al Azhar builds Islamic schools in many countries in the world, teachers and books are then sent to these schools from Al Azhar.
Muslim people from certain countries are given bursaries to study at Al Azhar and once they have completed their studies they are sent back to their own countries to work in the Mosques or schools.

Qur'an. My sole reason for memorising the Qur'an was out of sheer fear of Sheikh Ibrahim.

The Mosque in front of Al Azhar University

It was a case of Allah being the only one who could save me had I not memorised the specified readings for the day's recital. The lazy students were beaten as an example to the rest of the class.

I soon came to realise that the Sheikh received perverse pleasure from our pain. His cruelty reached a terrible climax when, in a frenzy of rage, Sheikh Ibrahim tied a disobedient student's legs together and hung him upside down like a slaughtered lamb and continuously whipped him first on the soles of his feet and then all over his body. I watched in horror as his feet swelled...

When I was twelve years old, I went to preparatory school. At this stage I had memorised the Qur'an completely.

I began my high school years with a lesson depicting the life of Mohammed. My subjects included doctrines of Islamic faith in the way of Al Emman Malek (which can be compared to a gospel in the Bible e.g.: Mark or Luke), analysis of the Qur'an as well as other prerequisite subjects such as Mathematics and Arabic but, naturally, all subjects had a strong Islamic slant.

Being a good student I graduated from preparatory school with excellent results. I must confess that the Islamic subjects I studied at school shaped my life. In particular a subject called the principals of Islamic belief which I studied for three successive years, affected me profoundly in that it fuelled my hate for Christianity. It planted in me a belief that Jesus or Isa as He is known in Islam was merely a prophet, not God incarnate and that Christians were sacrilegious, therefore they should be tortured and put to death or at least be given the chance to be converted to Islam.

If the Christians were to cling to their faith then the price was to be high: taxes and humility in the face of Islam. Evidently I began to detest all Christians with the one exception of the woman who breast-fed me: Omm William, who I felt was my true mother. Because of my devotion to her I used to delude myself into believing that she was in fact a Muslim in order to justify my love for her.

4. THE MONK' S ACCIDENT

There was a Christian monastery nearby called St Shenouda. The monks used to leave their cells and go into the city. I often saw them pass by our house and it was at the tender age of thirteen that I used to pelt them with stones, spit on them and curse them.

One day, one of the monks complained to my father about my insolent behaviour whereupon which he gave me a severe beating. This further increased my hatred for monks and I decided on revenge. I fabricated a small bomb by taking Calcium Oxide, adding water and sealing the mixture tightly in a bottle. I waited for the monk to pass as usual. I followed him secretly and inserted the bottle in the donkey's rectum. After a while the bottle exploded violently and the poor beast heaved throwing the monk off it's back.

As a result the monk was badly injured, requiring an ambulance and medical attention. During the first day of the monk's stay in hospital a policeman made enquiries about the incident. The monk regained consciousness on the second day but in spite of all the inquiries from the police, the monk refused to make a statement. He answered simply by saying it was an accident even though he knew who the culprit was.

Upon the monk's discharge from hospital, he paid a visit to our family home and told my parents that he was not angry with me.
He called me to his side: *'Mustafa!'*
I went to him, trembling.
He took me in his arms saying: *'I am not angry with you my son, but please I beg you not to do it again, neither to me nor to anyone else. I assure you that I love you and only ask that you love me in return.'*

I was deeply touched by the monk s behaviour towards me and weeping, I promised him that I would never do it again. I assured him that I loved him as he loved me. I asked for his forgiveness because I had sinned.
He replied: *'I forgave you before my operation.'*
As the monk left my home, all malice left me. From that day I changed my opinion towards monks and Christians. Seeing them in a new light, as humble, pure people of sound character.

5. THE WAY OF EL RAFFAIEYA[2]

One day I saw my classmate Sayed walking with an elderly man with a long white beard and green head covering. I asked Sayed about this man because he was different from the Sheikhs in Al Azhar. Sayed told me that this man was the Sheikh of Abouh Kouta, Sheikh of a Muslim sect called El Raffaieya. I was later to become a member of this sect and a disciple of this man.

When I asked him what the main teachings of this sect were, the Sheikh replied: *'It is the way to truth and the right way, my son. He who learns from me and becomes like me, for him the gates of paradise are opened and the gates of hell are forever shut. Everyone who is on the same path as I will receive a gift from Allah on the day he enters paradise. Yes Allah will praise us on this day saying; 'You are my cherished children, come into paradise. For each of you ten thousand houris[3].''*

Upon hearing this I expressed my delight to the Sheikh, asking him to show me the way to be like him.
The Sheikh replied: *'How old are you my boy ?'*
'Fifteen years old, Sir'
'Oh so you're the same age as your friend Sayed. The two of you are still young, not old men like me. You do understand that any member of El Raffaeiya has a gift from Allah - One thousand houris waiting in paradise for him. But for you and Sayed the gift of houris is increased by five hundred.'
'But why, Sir, is the number of houris so great for us? How can we live with such a great number of women in paradise ?' I enquired.
He answered me with: *'You ignorant boy there is nothing impossible for Allah, he will grant you the physical strength to sexually satisfy a thousand houris in one night.'*

---

[2] Raffaieya - This Islamic movement does not believe in Jihad in the use of violence to obtain goals, but rather they believe in only a spiritual Jihad against Satan. This movement was founded in the year 1100 by Sheikh Abehamid Al Gazali and his pupils, Sheikh Ibna' Arabee, Sheikh Sharanee and Sheikh Abe Azeed Al Boostami. This movement has many lines coming from it, for example: Teejaneya and Fefa-eya.

[3] Houris are women which are given to men in paradise as reward.

So I gladly believed the Sheikh and ceased to doubt his words. My adolescent mind of fifteen years was very attracted to this idea of a paradise filled with physical pleasure.
I heard Sayed saying to me: *'Come with us Mustafa, there's celebration now in the house of the chief Sheikh. This way the Sheikh can give you special guidance.'*
So I agreed and followed them.

When he actually arrived they encircled him, dancing around him hysterically. Whipped into an emotional frenzy, some fell to the ground exhausted. I saw how the chief Sheikh began to dance in a strange exaggerated fashion. He was so caught up in his strange dance that he was unaware that his green head covering had fallen off his head. Suddenly someone brought in poisonous snakes and scorpions! The people began to dance whilst teasing and provoking these animals. In my fear I began to scream.

Sheikh Abou Kouta said: *'Don't be scared, you are in God's presence and in our presence no harm will come to you.'*
He called to one of the men, asking him to bring snakes and scorpions. When the man reached us I screamed loudly. The Sheikh silenced me harshly, shouting, *'Stay where you are, keep your faith steadfast, so that your place in paradise will be assured! Take the snake and put it around your neck.'* Then he took a scorpion and threw it in my face. I fainted...

When I awoke I found myself on the lap of the Sheikh Abou Kouta. He was speaking gibberish that I did not understand. Then I heard him say to me, *'Thank Allah that you passed the test and secured for yourself a place in paradise. Come with me that I may give you direction.'* And again he began to speak in that strange unintelligible language: *'Ahmy hameesa uttmy tumeesa, hai kayoum hai'*

After this, he raised my head in his hands: *'Congratulations to the young Al Raffaeiya'*

And he gave the gift of selected Qur'an verses saying: *'Recite these verses in your house and in the mosque every day except for Thursday and Monday. On Thursday and Monday you and your four friends, Hassan, Shaeban and Ramadan will leave home at 2:30 am and go to the Muslim graveyard. Each of you must climb into a grave, alone, and sit in a corner reciting the selected verses of the Qur'an given to you and await the dawn prayers. When you hear the dawn prayers from the mosques, three of you must leave your graves, and go to the fourth person and after asking his permission, climb into his grave. One of you will be the Imam*[4] *and you must recite a special prayer in a strange tongue (the above-mentioned gibberish). Each of you must sit in a corner of the grave until sunrise upon which you must return home.'*

So when Thursday arrived, my friend Hassan woke me at 2:30 am: *'Wake up Mustafa, let's go to the cemetery.'*
I did the ritual cleansing that must precede every prayer, and my three friends and I made our way to the graveyard. As I walked, I felt the darkness, silence and fear engulfing us. We remembered that our Sheikh advised us to find comfort in certain Qur'anic verses when we are afraid and to recite them when we climbed into the graves.

Clambering into one of the graves, I found myself in utter darkness...

I began to recite my Qur'anic verses: *'In the name of Allah may no earthly or heavenly entity harm us.'*

I addressed the decaying inhabitants of the grave: *'You have preceded us into the grave where we shall one day follow. Peace be upon you, the dwellers of this place...'*

---

[4] An Imam is a leader in prayer.

'Peace be upon you, little one.' an invisible voice spoke to me. Suddenly a heavy man was standing before me.
'Who brought you to this place?' He demanded, grabbing me by the neck. He began choking me. Believing I was dead, he threw me aside and fled from the grave. I gazed at the little puddle of water on the ground just before I fainted...

Followers of El Raffaieya

I spent the rest of the night unconscious at the bottom of the grave. My friends had no idea where I was.

When I awoke, I found a naked corpse beside me, I estimated that he had been dead for at least two days. I realised that the aggressor who tried to kill me had robbed the corpse of the rich silk and satin coverings that were wrapped around the deceased.

I scrambled out of the grave and ran home, trembling. In front of our house I collapsed, very exhausted. A few of my brothers carried me into the house and put me on my bed.

As my mother was weeping, my father demanded: *'Where were you last night, and what happened to you?'*
I conveyed my story and my father swore at me: *'I will tie you to the bed and never allow you to leave this house!'*
He loudly cursed the El Raffaeya sect.

My three friends came a little later to enquire about me. With the appropriate courtesy, my father told them what had happened to me and ordered them to never again come near our home. *'...and if I ever see that Sheikh of yours, I will rip his head from his body!'*

That was the end of the connection with my friends and also with El Raffaeiya which enabled me to pay more attention to my studies.

6. CONCENTRATING ON MY STUDIES

At sixteen, I entered Al Azhar Secondary school. I was elected as class president in the first year of my studies. This was a great honour, as I did not only act as president for my own particular year-group, but also for every Azharic institute in Egypt. In the same year, I acted as co-ordinator for two sports teams at Al Azhar University, the Marathon team and the Basketball team. These two teams had beaten all of the eight Upper provinces. The final matches were to be played at the University of Cairo stadium. The games was against

Upper Egypt and North Egypt. The Basketball team won the Grand final and was awarded the coveted Cup of Egypt. The Marathon team came second and was awarded silver. As for myself, I came third in both high jump and long jump.

CHAPTER 2

1. THE INSULTING SHEIKH DOCTOR

After the completion of my high school years, I attended Al Azhar University in Cairo, studying Islamic History and Civilisations, in the faculty of Arabic Languages. On the very first day of lectures during the first lecture, the professor told us: *'What I tell you should be accepted as truth. I will not allow any form of class discussion. What I do not say is not worth knowing. Listen and obey and do not ask any questions.'*

I was disturbed about this philosophy and stood up and inquired: *'Oh Master Sheikh, how can there be teaching without questions?'*

'Where are you from, boy!' he demanded.

'From Egypt, Master Sheikh' I replied, not realising that it was the obvious answer.

'I know, but from where in Egypt!'

'From the Sayeed[5], Master, Sir.'

'So then you are an ignorant jackass!'

I was shocked. I did not think that I was misbehaving in any way and did not understand why this man was insulting me.

'Yes, I must be a donkey to leave the Sayeed and come here and be insulted!'

The class was silent. I decided on leaving, but as I reached the door, my adversary stopped me with: *'Stop, you animal, what's your name?'*

'It's no honour for me to tell you.' I replied coldly.

The professor was mad by now and in a frenzy he yelled: *'You stupid boy! Why do you think I asked for your name - to seduce your bloody mother? I need to know your name so I can cross it off the University list and throw you back into the streets, you vile boy.'*

I thought that it wasn't such a bad idea, but keeping my cool I asked him: *'Where do these words come from? From the Qur'an you teach or from Islamic teachings? Don't you fear Allah? What did the*

---

[5] Sayeed - Upper Egypt

people in Upper Egypt do to you that you compare them to animals?' With that I left the room going directly to the dean of the faculty.

The dean asked what happened and I explained the whole conflict with the Sheikh. The Sheikh was called into the office and asked for his side of the story. Immediately, as he sat down close to the dean, he pointed at me and said: *'This student should be expelled from the University and thrown in the street.'*
I couldn't believe that he still wouldn't cease. *'Even if you expelled me from the University, I'll never be thrown on the street because my father has great connections and can get me into any university in Egypt or any other country in the world. I am losing my patience with your insults and still you keep insulting me in front of the dean.'* Turning to the dean I continued: *'Sir, I left my comfortable home to receive an education at the greatest, most esteemed Islamic University in the world. I did not come here to be abused.'*

The dean, addressing the professor, said: *'Mustafa seems like a polite, intelligent student. In fact, he reminds me of your son. I'm sure he does not have any bad intentions.'*
The Sheikh reluctantly forgave me but made it clear that it was only because of the dean's influence.

When the Sheikh had left, the dean asked me to stay for a cup of tea and tried to persuade me that the Sheikh was in fact a very pious man and a clever teacher. *'Take him to be a father figure,'* he said, *'who only wishes to correct you, not insult you.'*
I allowed myself to be swayed by the dean's words and started feeling more positive about the situation.

Although this incident taught me the way of silence and submission, I gained respect from my peers as well as the academic staff. I was known around campus as the feisty boy with the sense of justice. Sayeedy people was also viewed in a different light.

The Black Stone in the centre of the Ka'aba: When Muslims pray it is always in the direction of the Black Stone

2. GRADUATING WITH A DEGREE - BEGINNING MY MASTERS

I finished my third and fourth years at University successfully. In my final year I was graded second best out of six thousand students.

After my degree, I served the required year in the defence force. Strangely, this was the most quiet, stable period of my life.

Upon returning from the defence forces, I confirmed my degree and started working towards a Master's degree. The subject of my thesis was *'The reign of the Heir Over the Islamic Kingdom in the period of Ammaweya.'* I started my research with enthusiasm. As part of my research I had to travel abroad to many Eastern and Western countries. I was awarded my Master's degree in 1990.

The price I paid for my degree, however, was further disillusionment with Islam. I found the Islamic history, from its commencement to date, to be filled with violence and bloodshed without any

worthwhile ideology or sense or decency. I asked myself: *'What religion would condone such destruction of human life?'*
Based on that, I began to see that the Muslim people and their leaders were perpetrators of violence.

In the face of my growing knowledge, I myself became a lost soul...

3. NEW QUR'AN IN IRAN

After the completion of my Masters degree I was offered a position at the university as a lecturer. This provided me with more opportunity to search for true peace and truth.

My search led me to many foreign countries, such as Tehran, the birthplace of Khomeine.

I found a Qur'an in Iran and as I was reading it I noticed differences to that which I memorised. I noted a whole chapter, Al Walaya, containing five verses, that was different to that of the Qur'an I knew. Upon inspection I noted that this Qur'an in Iran consisted of 115 chapters where the Qur'an in Egypt and Saudi Arabia contained only 114 chapters.

This was the last straw, the last breath of the faith I had in Islam and the Qur'an.

4. MEETING WITH MY PEERS AT AL AZHAR

When my professors and peers at the university learned that I had forsaken Islamic teachings, a meeting was arranged in order for them to establish what was wrong with me. Upon their inquiries I spoke to them without hiding a single fact: *'I cannot say anymore that the Qur'an comes directly from heaven or from Allah. I have conviction for what I am saying. The Qur'an was written by the Arabs but I do not have any proof that Mohammed wrote it. Yet I have proof that the Qur'an is not from heaven, but from human thoughts.'*

These were very blasphemous words in their opinion and they spat in my face. One of them cursed me saying: *'You blasphemer. I swear you are a bastard.'*
Another shouted: *'You, a student of Al Azhar! So we (students) are taught by blasphemers and non-believers like you!'*

I used to feel that the people who worked with me at university were different to me, but at that moment it finally came to truth.

Even though I did not accept any other faith, my superiors as well as the principal was informed immediately. They filed a severe report about me and I was formally expelled from AL Azhar on 17 December 1991.

Mohammed's Mosque showing the famous green dome

5. THE PRISON AND PERSECUTION

The university management also contacted the Department of Islamic Social Ministry asking them to release me from duty as Imam in the Mosque of Amas Ebn Malek in Gisa city, in the province of Gisa. I was to immediately stop all my activities in this Mosque.

The department of Egyptian police were contacted very quickly and I was arrested in my house and taken to the Department for Highest

Government Security in the centre of Cairo and put into prison to be questioned. Little did I know that I would stay in that cell for three days without food or water.

With me in the cell were two Muslim men, one a Palestinian and the other an Egyptian who were both accused of terrorist acts as members of the Jihad fundamentalists. Every day I was asked by the Egyptian man why I was there. I refused to answer because I was afraid that he would kill me if he knew that I had left Islam. After three days I told him that I was a teacher at Al Azhar university and an Imam in the Amas Ebn Malek Mosque. He concluded that I was linked with the Islamic movement in Egypt and thought that this was the reason for my being in prison. Immediately he gave me some food and water that he was given by his visitors and told me that he was warned by the police not to give me anything. He then added: *'I am pleased with you, for you are my brother in Islam. I am going to give you whatever I have, from now on we will share it together.'*

On the fourth day the intense investigation started. They started by hitting me, swearing and insulting me. The sergeant in charge of the investigation asked in surprise: *'From the very first day you were forbidden to eat any food, we left you to die from hunger because you are a kaffir*[6] *- the Islamic Law demands your death. But tell me, what is the reason that you did not become weak? Who gave you food?'*
I answered: *'God is the only one who sent me food every day.'*
The sergeant probed for further details: *'From inside the prison or from outside?'*
'From inside.' I answered.
With that he barked: *'We have warned the other prisoners not to give you food!'*

The investigation lasted four days. This included trying to make me talk by branding me with a red-hot iron from a fire placed on various parts of my body, extinguishing cigarettes on my lips, arms and in

---

[6] Kaffir in Arabic is the word used for an unbeliever.

my mouth. They poured cold water out onto my head and kept swearing at me and insulting me.
On the seventh day in prison, the cell mate who gave me food learned that I was accused of leaving Islam and converting to Christianity[7] (which at this stage I did not do yet). Immediately, my generous helper jumped up and attacked me. Just then the police came into the cell with a previously written order for my transferral to the Calipha prison in Southern Cairo...

The week I spent in Calipha prison turned out to be a much more relaxed time because I became friends with Colonel Aosamah who was the prison guard. He had a brother who was killed by Muslim fundamentalists in Asiute City in South Egypt. Aosamah could never understand why Muslim people would kill each other and then say that it comes from God. I became good friend with Aosamah and he told me that he had seen many people who were imprisoned by the Egyptian government, who had done nothing wrong, or who had been killed by these Muslim people without having done anything.

I was set free and yet I had not at this time converted to Christianity. I did not understand which power protected me and who had opened the doors for me. Only after having a personal meeting with Christ did I understand how God had a hand in my life, from the time that He sent me a Christian woman to drink milk from, up to the time that He opened the prison doors to me.

6. ONE YEAR WITHOUT BELIEF IN ANY GOD

When I returned home after leaving jail, my father could not understand what had happened to me. He inquired at the police, asking for information about his son. The report they gave him was: *'We have received a fax from Al Azhar University accusing your son of leaving Islam, but after an interrogation of fifteen days, we found no evidence to support it.'*

---

[7] The penalty for converting to Christianity from the Islam faith, according to Islamic Law is death.

My father was relieved to hear this but still upset with the decision of the university, he told me: *'My son, we do not need the university or it's salary, come and help me in my factory.'* I agreed and started immediately as sales director.

For one year I had every materialistic thing I needed, but yet I experienced a deep tiredness. I had no God to pray to, to call to, to live for. I called to the Creator, but I had no idea who he was. Was He the God of the Muslims, of the Christians or the Jews, or was he one of the many gods of the far east? Or was he some animal - like the Cow of the Hindus? I did not know, I had no knowledge or direction to turn to, to reach this God. On Fridays[8] I used to walk the streets, laughing by myself as I saw the Muslims leaving the Mosques after prayer, asking myself: *'How long will these people persist in their way before they realise what I have come to realise about Islam?'* I heard the Imams calling out their messages of criticism against the Government and the unbelievers and I was filled with disgust as I realised that they used God for their own business deals.

During that whole year I suffered from constant headaches. I was always burdened and in search of the true God. Deep in my soul I believed that this world needed the true God, but I had never dreamt that it was the Hand of Jesus Christ that was leading me to the end of my search[9].

---

[8] Friday is the Muslims day of rest - like Sunday for Christians or Saturday for Jews.

[9] Jeremiah 29:13 Seek me and you will find me when you search for me with all your heart.

CHAPTER 3

WHY DID I LEAVE ISLAM?

1. MY LIFE WITH THE QUR'AN

I mentioned in a previous chapter that I had finished memorising the whole Qur'an at the age of twelve. Thus it can be said that I was raised on and with the Qur'an, which constituted the foundation of my Islamic beliefs. As a result of that, I came to consider 'Destiny' an important axis on which my whole life revolved.

'Destiny' in Islam is what brought me to this world in order to be tried. The Qur'an says: *'Verily we created man from a drop of mingled sperm in order to try him: So we gave him (the gifts) of hearing and sight. We showed him the way: whether he be grateful or ungrateful.' S76:2-3*

'Destiny' is what fixed the years of my life at a certain number of years, I cannot exceed it or reduce it because the Qur'an says: *'To every people is a term appointed: when their term is reached, not an hour can they cause delay, nor (an hour) can they advance.'*
S7:34

'Destiny' is what dictates my fortune in life, which is in the hands of God who has full control over it, and there is nothing that I can do about it: *'Gracious is God to his servants, He gives sustenance to whom He pleases and has power and can carry out His will.'*
S47:19

Happiness and misery are also eternally determined for us: *'The day it arrives, no soul shall speak except by His leave: of those (gathered) some will be wretched and some will be blessed.'*
S11:105

In a speech by 'Abdullah Ibn Massoud', he says: *'The miserable is he who has experienced misery in his mother's womb.'*
Igas al-Qur'an Volume 1, page 195

This is in regard to the length of our life, our fortune, happiness or misery. All these have been predetermined and established according to the destiny that has been decreed on all Muslims.

On the other hand, with regard to obedience, believing, and committing sin, I have no choice on them either. The Qur'an tells me that they have been prescribed on me since eternity, and I cannot change anything or choose something that God doesn't want me to have. The Qur'an says: *'By the soul and proportion and order given to it and its enlightenment as to its wrong and its right; truly he succeeds that purfies it, and he fails that corrupts it.' S91:7-10*

According to that, it was God who led me into sin and into righteousness. But it is not up to me to choose or to decide on my own. Why? It is because God alone has the power according to His decision on me and on every Muslim. On each soul, He prescribes life or death, sin or guidance, and nobody can change that. The Qur'an says: *'And we have destined for them intimate companions (of like nature), who made alluring to them what was before them and behind them; and the sentence amongst the previous generations of Jinns and men, who have passed away, is proved against them." S41:25*

'When we decide to destroy a population, we (first) send a definite order to those among them who are given the good things of this life to transgress, so that the word is proved true against them : then (it is) we destroy them utterly." S17:16

According to another reading of the above verse, the word 'order' would mean princes or rulers. In other words, God would make those people princes and rulers so that they may transgress as they rule, then God will have a reason to destroy them utterly.

God also says in the Qur'an, *'God's plan is that He will give them no portion in the hereafter.' S3:176.*

As to the soul that God chose to grant it obedience and faith, the Qur'an says: *'As one whose heart God has opened to Islam so that he has received enlightenment from God." S39:22*
'He punishes whom He pleases, and He grants mercy to whom He pleases.' S29:21

Thus there is nothing in God that man can covet.

Ali ibn Abi Talib was quoted as saying: Bokary Faliam Volume 3, page 216: *'From this, I concluded that God is the one who makes all the decisions. At the same time He helps, inspires and facilitates the faithful to hold onto their faith. Then He is pleased with them and He enters them into His paradise.*

On the other hand, He leads the wrong-doers into a life of sin, corruption, disbelief and associating partners with Him. There would be no reconciliation between the two groups; the faithful and the wrong-doers."

The Qur'an says: *'Accordingly, no soul can do anything other than what has been prescribed to her, still it is her responsibility to which she will give an account in the day of judgement.'*

Based on all that, the Sunnis concluded the following: *'Everything that happens in this world whether it be good or bad, comes according to God's will. It is written from the beginning of times on the preserved plate. Its contents are final and unchangeable. God has not only made the decision as to what every person will encounter in life whether it be happiness or misery, He also prescribed man's faith and obedience, or infidelity and disobedience, and consequently He prescribed what will happen in the hereafter, whether it be eternal happiness in Paradise or eternal torment in Hell-fire."*

The Determinists concluded: *'Man is predetermined and is not a free agent in what he does. This is because all man's deeds are prescribed on him since eternity."*
In light of all this, it is clear that destiny, whether it be good or bad, is one of the basis of faith in Islam, and the one that determines everything in the Muslim's life.

This led me to serious and important questions:

1 If God has already predetermined all deeds in my life and I don't have the free will or choice in anything, is it fair that He will hold me accountable on the day of judgement for the deeds that He prepared for me and led me and helped me to commit?

And then there is a more serious question:

2 If God has already decided everything in man's life, and if He also uses demons to carry out this scenario of predeterminism, why then does He send Apostles, Prophets and Books to man?

By every available means, I tried to find a logical explanation to the following Qur'anic verse, but to no avail: *'And he whose sight is dim to the remembrance of the Beneficent (Allah), We (Allah) assign unto him a devil who becometh his comrade; And lo! they surely turn them from the way of Allah, and yet they deem that they are rightly guided; Till, when he cometh unto Us (Allah), he saith (unto his comrade): Ah, would that between me and thee there were the distance of the two horizons - an evil comrade! And it profiteth you not this day, because you did wrong, that ye will be sharers in the doom." S43:36-39.*

It is very hard for me to read something that says God, the creator, is an antagonistic God, unloving to man. It is difficult to understand that God works through demons to mislead man. However, I find another Qur'anic verse that says, whether you accept it or not, it is God who says it: *' And whomsoever it is Allah's will to guide, He expanded his bosom unto the Surenderer, and whomsoever it is His will to send astray, He maketh his bosom close and narrow as if he were engaged in sheer ascent. Thus Allah layeth ignominy upon those who believe not." S6:125.*

If you ask me why? I tell you because the Qur'an says *'... -If Allah willed, He could have brought them all together to the guidance- So be not thou among the foolish ones." S6:35* and because it says *'...Lo! Allah changeth not the condition of a folk until they (first) change that which is in their hearts; and if Allah willeth misfortune for a folk there is none that can repel it, nor have they a defender beside Him." S13:11.*
And all that because *'Allah giveth life and causeth death; and Allah is Seer of what ye do." S3:156.*

I found myself worshipping a god that I cannot trust, or feel that He loves me and wants to half my human weakness.

I found my religion built on unstable ground that cannot stand against the wind of truth. I started to question myself in all these issues which exploded in front of me. The good Lord used all these doubts to provide me with an opportunity to be candid with myself. I started to ask myself many questions:

1 How can I worship a god who didn't show Himself, or His mercy, love and care to me?
2 How can I worship a god who has among his attributes deceit, delusion and trickery?
3 How can I settle down and be at peace while my religion doesn't give a guarantee of deliverance from Hell-fire into eternity?
4 How can I live my life through a religion that doesn't explain anything to me concerning my future? A religion that makes me live wandering about like a sheep who is being led to slaughter without knowing it?
5 How can I live with a religion that doesn't put an end to the burden of sin which I have been carrying on my shoulders since the day I was born?

6. How can I live with a religion which is based on fear? (It makes me fear the torment of the grave, fear the day of judgement because there is no advocate or assurance of forgiveness.)

There were many questions attacking my mind and almost caused it to explode.

2. PEACE AND ISLAM

After I enrolled in al-Azhar University and specialising in the Islamic history and culture, I discovered that this study of Islam in its application in the different countries of the world will make a Muslim confused about his religion.

In other words, it made me want a full clarification about what Islam is all about. Is it a religion that calls for love and tolerance towards others and leave others to exercise freedom of choice regarding religion? Or is it a religion that prevents freedom of religion and forces others into believing in it?

At first I went to the Qur'an trying to find the answer. I was so happy to find a big number of Qur'anic verses that call for love, peace and freedom of choice. Here are some examples:

S5:105 - 'O ye who believe! Ye have charge of your own souls."
S2:256 - 'There is no compulsion in religion"
S2:272 - 'And whatsoever good thing ye spend, it is for yourselves, when ye spend not save in search of Allah's countenance; and whatsoever good thing ye spend, it will be repaid to you in full, and you will not be wronged."
S20:44 - 'And speak unto him a gentle word, that peradventure he may heed or fear."
S3:144 - 'He who turneth back (away from Islam) doth not hurt Allah, and Allah will reward the thankful."

I also went to inquire from the Qur'an about the exact task that God has charged Mohammed with. I found that God has only charged him with the task of conveying the message and warning people; that is to convey God's message and to warn them about the consequences of their non-belief in Him. When I discovered that there were full Suras and many verses in the Qur'an that call for that, I was satisfied in my heart. The following are only examples of these verses:

S3:144 - 'Mohammed is but a messenger..."

S42:48 - '...We(Allah) have not sent thee as a warder over them. Thine is only to convey (the message)."

S18:56 - 'Lo! thou (O Muhammed) guidest not whom thou lovest, but Allah guidest whom He will."

I was following the Islamic publications and broadcasts which were directed towards non-Muslims for the purpose of spreading Islam. I noticed that they present Islam in a fancy wrapper. They make it look good. They talk about Islam through love, peace and tolerance. They emphasize that the world is in need of salvation from Islam.

Even the students who come from the western world and study in al-Azhar University, when I ask them how they perceive Islam in their countries, they always say as a loving, peaceful and merciful religion.

I always asked myself, what if those students were from Iraq, Iran, Yemen, Egypt, Afghanistan or Lebanon..... I don't think they would say the same thing. This is because they will never forget the millions of people who have been killed at the hands of their Muslim brothers. No-one can forget these streams of blood which have been running through the Islamic history when Muslims starts killing Muslims for reasons such as Jihad, struggle for the Caliphat, sectarian strife, Apostasy war and tribal disputes, etc.

I kept studying and researching the Qur'an and the Hadith and its related commentaries. I must acknowledge that it is not easy to study all that, but you have to because you cannot come up with a definite conclusion unless you concur with all these commentaries and regulations.

After much consideration, I concluded that the first stage of Islam, the peaceful, merciful and just Islam, has already ended. Now I am thrown into a different stage, a strange and cruel stage, a hazardous and dangerous road where you find corpses and limbs scattered on every side. Blood runs like streams from the top of its heights. Millions of Muslims are being killed at the hands of their Muslim brethren. I found millions of children rendered orphans, hundreds of thousands of women become widows after losing their husbands.

My dear reader, I would like to give you just one little example from the Islamic history to prove my point.

In the year 36 of Hijira, Aysha, the wife of the prophet of Islam, had a dispute with the prophet's cousin Ali ibn abi Talib. As a result, she went to fight him at el-Basra in Iraq. The battle lasted three days, during which ten thousand Muslims died. After the battle she and Ali participated in the prayer for those who had been killed. When it was hard for any Muslims to understand this, a Muslim asked Aysha, *'How come the people who are killed belong to opposing camps? Who will enter Paradise and who will be led to Hell-fire?'* Her answer was that each one of them went to Paradise. (See "Al-Bidaia Wal-Nihaia by Ibn-Kathir Volume 7, page 242). But who can accept such a statement.

I have also discovered Muslim clergy who became military commanders and who let troops of holy warriors and sanctioned war, the killing of people and the destruction of buildings.

My dear reader, please don't shiver as I tell you that some of these new military commanders were religious leaders, professors and preachers. They issued sanctions to kill non-Muslims, to steal their money in order to finance these battles that they waged against their Muslim brethren whether they be citizens or governments.

One example is my professor Sheikh Abdullah Al-Samawi who led the organisation called "Al-Shawkyeen" in Egypt. He issued a religious opinion (sanction) that is lawful in Islam to steal the gold that belongs to Christian goldsmiths and also to kill them. He said that it is also lawful to steal automobiles from downtown Cairo and take them to El-Fayoum desert where they take them apart and send the parts back to Cairo to be sold and with that money, buy weapons that are used in their struggle against the government.

Another example is my professor Sheikh Omar Abdul Rohman who is now in prison in the United States for conspiring to explode the World Trade Centre in New York. Sheikh Omar Abdul Rohman taught me the subject 'Qur'an commentary' in Al-Azhar University. He left his job at the university to lead the two organisations "Jihad" and "Gamaa al-Islamia". This Sheikh used to attack and curse the leaders of the Egyptian government as well as other Arab leaders. He used to swear in the name of Allah that all these governments, from Baghdad to Rabat in Morocco, are all infidels who abandoned Islam and it is the duty of the citizens of all these

Sheikh Omar Abdul Rohman holding a copy of the Qur'an in Jail

countries to fight and overthrow them and establish an Islamic government.

Once I made a comment to him that the line of Jihad and killing is not the only line in Islam and that there are many Suras and verses in the Qur'an that talk about peace, love and forgiveness. I asked him why he is only holding onto the line of Jihad and killing. He answered saying, *'Listen my brother, there is a whole Sura (chapter) called al-Anfal (Prisoners of War), there is no Sura called Peace.'* He added, *"Jihad and killing is the head of Islam. If you take it out, you cut off the head of Islam.'*

I left my professor Sheikh Omar and turned back to the Qur'an to study this serious matter. After much studying of all the passages that talk about Jihad, and referring to the opinion of prominent Muslim scholars trying to explore its legitimacy, I found that the Islamic Fikh (legal opinion) has established a definition of Jihad as follows: *'It is fighting anybody who stands in the way of spreading Islam. Or fighting anyone who refuses to enter into Islam.' S8:39*
I found that the Qur'an discusses Jihad in detail. It classified Jihad into many topics. For instance, the Qur'an says the following about Jihad:

1. Jihad is a trade. *'Let those who fight in the way of Allah who sell the life of this world for the other. Whoso fighteth in the way of Allah, be he slain or be he victorious, on him We (Allah) shall bestow a vast reward." S4:74*
2. The call to Jihad. *S4:71-104; S 8:60-65*
3. The sanction of Jihad. *S4:88; S47:4; S9:123; S8:39-60*
4. The warning of taking 'people of the Book (Bible/Old Testament)' (Christians and Jews) as friends, and the call to fight them. *'O ye who believe! Take not the Jews and Christians for friends....." S5:51 see also S5:51-57; S4:89*
5. People of the Book (Bible/Old Testament) are cowards. *S48:29*
6. Condemning those who refuse Islam's call to fight people of the Book (Christians and Jews). *'And those who believe say: If only a Surah were revealed! But when a decisive Surah is*

revealed and war is mentioned therein, thou seest those in whose hearts is a disease looking at thee with the look of men fainting unto death. Therefore woe unto them!" S47:20

7. The call to stand firm and not to retreat. *'O ye who believe! When ye meet and army, hold firm and think of Allah much, that ye may be successful." S8:45*
8. Warning against retreat. *'Whoso on that day turn their back on them, unless manoeuvring for battle or intent to join a company, he truly hath incurred wrath from Allah, and his habitation will be hell, a hapless journey's end." S8:16-17*
9. Threats against those who don't participate in Jihad and fighting. *'And they said: Go not forth in the heat! Say (unto them): The heat of hell is more intense of heat, if they but understood." S9:81*
10. The necessity of punishing those who abandon Jihad and fighting. *S9:83-86*
11. Scolding those who didn't participate in Jihad. *S4:77*
12. The consequences of rejecting Islam. *'Lo, those who disbelieve and turn from the way of Allah and then die disbelievers, Allah will surely not pardon them." S47:34*
13. Killing whoever rejects Islam. *'...If they keep not aloof from you, nor offer you peace nor hold their hands, then take them and kill them wherever ye find them.Against such We (Allah) have given you clear warrant." S4:91*
14. The reason behind legalizing Jihad. *'And verily We shall try you till We know those of you who strive hard (for the cause of Allah) and steadfast, and till We test your record." S47:31*
15. Those who participate in Jihad are better than those who don't. *S4:95*
16. Using harshness and making homeless Jews and Christians when fighting with them. *S8:57*
17. Warning against abandoning Islam. *S5:54-56*
18. A call to Muslims to accept God and Mohammed's call to Jihad. *S8:24-36*
19. The participation of Angels in Jihad. *S8:12-13*
20. Inciting Muslims into fighting. *S8:56*

21. God fights with Muslims. *S47:35*

After I finished this serious study which made the Qur'an's philosophy of Jihad and Holy War clear to me, I found out that the goal of Jihad is fighting whoever stands in the way of the Islamic call. This is a general statement that can be applied to any person or country that stands against Islam whether they be the traditional enemy of Islam such as the Jews and the Christians, or the followers of other religions. Even this can be applied to Muslims themselves which explains the hidden secret for hundreds of years: Why Muslims are fighting their Muslim brethren, and why a Muslim country is fighting another Muslim country. This is in contrast to what Mohammed said according to al-Bukhari *If two Muslims meet each other with their swords, the killer and the one who is killed are both destined to Hell-fire.'*

Brother or sister, I will now take you on a short tour across the Islamic history from the very beginning to the present time. This history tore me apart from the time I started studying it until I became an instructor who taught it in al-Azhar University and ten other Islamic universities in different Islamic countries. You will see how Muslims jumped on each other trying to kill one another.

1. Abu-Bakr fighting the Muslims for refusing to pay alms. History says that Abu Bakr used the sword to kill tens of thousand of Muslims.
2. Ali Ibn Abu Talib fights with Aysha, the second wife of Mohammed in Basra in Iraq in the year 36 Hijira. This battle lasted only three days during which ten thousand Muslims were killed.
3. The attack of Muslim rebels on the third Caliph Uthman and their breaking into his house where they killed him as he was reciting the Qur'an.
4. The war between Ali Ibn Abu Talib the fourth Caliph and Moawia Ibn Abu Sofyan the prince of Sham in the battle of Seffein and the killing of tens of thousands on both sides.

5. The Ommiad dynasty under the leadership of Yazid Ibn Moawia killing Al-Hussein the son of Mohammed's daughter and the slaughtering of his entire household in the city of Karbellaa in Iraq.

6. The Abbasside dynasty, the family of Mohammed's uncle, waged war against the Ommiad dynasty in which they wiped them out completely, to the point that only one man of that family remained alive in Arabian land. His name is Soliman Ibn Abdelmalek because he was a friend to the Abbasside prince, Abu El Abbas al-Safah (Safah means shedder [of blood] because he shed the blood of many people from the Ommiad dynasty). Soliman was also killed as a result of 2 lines of a poem an Abbasside poet recited against him when the poet found the Abbasside prince eating with Soliman. The poet read his poem to the prince urging him to kill Soliman the Ommiad. The poem said, *'Don't be deceived by what you see from certain people, What is hidden inside is a terrible ailment indeed, Take your sword out and stop your amnesty, Until you don't find a person from the Ommiad dynasty.'*

Another man of the Ommiad dynasty named Abdel Rahman al-Dakhel, fled to Andalosia in Spain. Because there was no-one left from the Ommiad family, the Abbasside went to the Ommiad graves and dug them up.

And let's have a look at our modern history:

1. The war between Iraq and Iran, the two Muslim countries. In this war that lasted over 8 years, over two million Muslim youths were killed and over three million became handicapped.
2. The slaughter of 'Black Ailool' in which Jordan killed thousands of Palestinians in the streets of Jordan after dragging them behind their tanks.
3. The war between north and south Yemen and the killing from both sides under the command of Abdullah Saleh and Ali Salem al-Beid.

4. The fighting between Muslims in Afghanistan after establishing the Islamic government there. The killing continues until now.
5. Libyan Muslims under the command of Moammar al-Kaddafi, and how they killed tens of thousands of Muslim people of Chad. I have visited the battlefield myself and have seen these towns in North Chad (Provinces of Ozo, Ozanka and Dome Valley.)
6. The slaughter in Hama and Halab in Syria, and the slaughter of the Syrian prison 'Tadmar', when President Hafez al-Assad, the Muslim, killed tens of thousands from the Muslim Brethren group.
7. The famous slaughtering that the late Gamal Abdul Nasser conducted against the Muslim brethren group, including their leader Sayed Quotb.

After this brief outline my dear reader, I believe you can understand my confusion and perplexity. I found myself lost in a complex Islamic philosophy. Once it tells me that it came for mercy, forgiveness and peace, and another time it tells me that Jihad is the only way to enter Paradise, even if this Jihad means the killing of a Muslim at the hand of his Muslim brother which you have seen from our brief review of the Islamic history.

CHAPTER 4
MY MEETING WITH THE PHARMACIST

1. WHAT AM I DOING WITH THIS BIBLE?

One day, suffering from a severe headache, I went to a pharmacy to buy some medicine. I got aquatinted with the owner, a Christian woman who impressed me with her high standard of education and exceptional character. She invited me to return because she said that I was different to all the Muslim people she had met before.

I did go a second time and met her husband at the pharmacy, he was a veterinarian. The pharmacist inquired about my life and I told her that I was mentally and emotionally weary because I felt lost. She was surprised at this statement: *'But you are a member of the most respected Muslim University in Egypt. Both your brother, the Geology professor, and your father, a wealthy businessman, are very respected people in the community. I thought you had it all and there weren't any problems!'*

'This is true,' I replied *'But after I discovered falsehoods in their dogmas, I no longer believe my home and family was built on a foundation of truth. I felt naked in my beliefs, because I had always clothed myself in the lies of Islam. I found that my faith was not only shaken, it had completely dissolved! How can I fill the emptiness in my heart? I asked myself how one can retrieve faith where there is none.'*

'One sure can.' She replied.

'How can that be?' I asked.

'The false religion can be cast aside freely but real faith, real truth can only be bought by a yearning notwithstanding persecution. Do you believe this Mustafa?'

'Please help me' I said softly.

She asked: *'Have you ever read the Bible?'*

'No, but I'll try' I replied.

She gave me her own personal Bible: *'Take it, read it, then come back and tell me what you've found.'*

I agreed and with a book I never believed in before, I returned home.

2. ONE NIGHT WITH JESUS CHRIST

I open the Bible at random. My eyes fell on Matthew 5:38-44: *'You have heard what was said: "An eye for an eye and a tooth for a tooth." But I tell you not to resist an evil person. But whoever slaps you on your right cheek, turn the other to him also... and pray for those who hate you, and pray for those who spitefully use you and persecute you.'*

Upon reading these words, my whole body began trembling. It was impossible that these words was inspired by mere mortals, as the Muslims believe! Immediately, I thought about the Qur'an I'd spent my whole life studying - not once did I find words as inspirational as this! The Qur'an speaks only about the matter at hand: If one beats you, beat him more severely.

I started reading at nine in the evening until the early hours of the next day. I forgot about Islam, even about my life. I only wanted to read and know more. That first night, I read the Gospel of Matthew as well as The Acts of the Apostles.

With dawn breaking, the dawn of a new life broke for me...

Early that morning I gave my heart to Jesus Christ. After reading the truth in the pages of the Bible, I could easily compare it to what I had learned from the Qur'an. There was no doubt left in my mind when I finally decided to pray to the true God.

3. WHY I ACCEPTED JESUS CHRIST

I accepted the Lord Jesus Christ because I found His caring hands surrounding me from the beginning. When one door closes, many doors open up.

Wasn't it His hand that has sent the Christian lady neighbour who breastfed me when I was a little baby, this at a time when I refused to be fed by all the Muslim women in our family? Also, isn't He the loving God whom the monk worshipped, the monk to whom I caused the severe injury? After spending a whole month in hospital, he came to our house, not to take revenge, but to forgive. Who taught the monk this kind of forgiveness? Isn't He the loving God, the Lord Jesus Christ who gave Himself as a sacrifice to die on the cross in order to grant us forgiveness and eternal life?

Who gave me food inside prison when the police decided to deprive me of food until I died of hunger , because I was considered an infidel who deserved to die?

Isn't He the one who stood by me and led me to the truth which was hidden from me for a long time?

I would now like to point to the Bible which gave me all the answers that I was searching for all my life. How did the Bible introduce itself to me, a Muslim academic researcher, as God's holy word inspired from Him above? There were no preachers, monks or pastors who tried to prove to me that the Bible alone, and not the Qur'an is God's word. Nothing like this happened at all. Jesus was the one who called me to Him and glorified Himself in me.

One time I asked myself: *'Mustafa, what would you do to be in a healthy relationship with God and man?'* What a surprise to find the Bible giving me the speedy and satisfying answer. It is written in Acts 16 : 30, 31 *'He then brought them out and asked, "Men, what must I do to be saved?" They replied, "Believe in the Lord Jesus, and you will be saved - you and your household."'*

I must then find out how to be saved. So the Bible came up with the answer in Acts 3 : 19 *'Repent, then, and turn to God, so that your sins may be wiped out, that times of refreshing may come from the Lord.'*

At this point I started to ask myself: *'How about sin, Mustafa?'* About what sin does the Bible talk? My knowledge about sin came from the Qur'an, which says that when a person commits sin, he must be punished according to the sin he committed. For example, if you commit adultery while you are married, the punishment is to be death by stoning. I said to myself that if the Bible talks about sin in this sense, there is nothing new then.

What a big surprise to me when I found the Bible's point of view is completely different to that of the Qur'an. I found the Bible analysing sin in a wonderful way throughout both the Old and New Testaments. In Romans 3 : 17, 18, 23, it says *'and the way of peace they do not know.' 'There is no fear of God before their eyes.' 'for all have sinned and fall short of the glory of God'* and in Galatians 22 : 3, it says It also says in Psalm 14 : 2, 3 *'The Lord looks down from heaven on the sons of men to see if there are any who understand, any who seek God. All have turned aside, they have together become corrupt; there is no one who does good, not even one.'* And it explains the issue in Romans 5 : 12 *'Therefore just as sin entered the world through one man, and death through sin, and in this way death came to all men, because all sinned'*

I came up with a clear explanation from these passages as to the reasons that led man to live in sin in this world. My mind almost exploded as I was trying to figure out why man lives like this and why evil runs in man's blood.

The Bible gave me the answer to all these questions. The reader may go to the epistle of Romans to see how the Bible explained how the relationship between man and sin started and how sin brought death on the human race. God's love to the world made Him do that great deed with which He put an end to man's lost life as a result of sin. He did this by sending His beloved son, the Lord Jesus Christ, to give Himself as sacrifice for all the sins of the human race.

John 3 : 16 *'For God so loved the world that he gave his one and only Son, that whoever believes in him shall not perish but have eternal life.'*

Isaiah 53 : 3 - 6 *He was despised and rejected by men, a man of sorrows, and familiar with suffering. Like one from whom men hide their faces he was despised, and we esteemed him not. Surely he took up our infirmities and carried our sorrows, yet we considered him stricken by God, smitten by him, and afflicted. But he was pierced for our transgressions, he was crushed for our iniquities; the punishment that brought us peace was upon him, and by his wounds we are healed. We all, like sheep, have gone astray, each of us has turned to his own way; and the Lord has laid on him the iniquity of us all.'*

4. THE POWER OF THE BIBLE

There was no book in the world that was exposed to so as much criticism and attacks as the Bible. In spite of that, I found that followers of Jesus are not bothered by it.

When I asked the lady pharmacist about the reason, she told me because it is not our battle. I asked her why this is so, *'it is your book that you believe in, how come you don't defend it and sacrifice your life for it?'* She answered in a brilliant way that left me dumbfounded. She said that the Bible is God's word and God is not in need of man to defend His word, God it able to defend Himself.

I found out that the steadfastness of the Bible is the biggest proof that it is the word of God which no-one can kill or stop.

Another thing amazed me, how the Bible was a trap that caught everybody who collided with it. Here are some examples:

1. Paul the Apostle: His name was Saul and he had power to kill everyone who believed in Jesus Christ. He participated in killing Steven, the first martyr in Christianity. He was a learned man in the Jewish religion and Greek philosophy, but he was

changed to Paul the Apostle, the greatest preacher and servant of the Gospel. What is the secret of this radical change? Isn't it the effectiveness of the living Holy Word of God?

2. Dionamius the Ariobogian: He was a member of the house of representatives for the city of Athens, the city of philosophy. He was also a scientist in astronomy and philosophy. This man was converted to Christianity by Paul the Apostle.

3. Athinagoris: He was the dean of the school of philosophy in Alexandria (the largest school of philosophy at that time.) He was one of the founders of the modern Platonic creed. This man became a Christian and a student of the Cross which is ignorance according to human wisdom.
4. Arianos: The ruler of Insena in upper Egypt, who tortured thousands of Christians, and in the end, he became a martyr of the Cross of Jesus Christ.
5. Augustine : He devoted his life to attacking the Bible but then became a Christian and carried the Cross and became one of the greatest commentators of the Bible.

The Bible was persecuted by every earthly power and human wisdom but remained the trap which has caught all of them and transformed the evil doers to saints. It changed the arrogants into humble people and its adversaries into those who defend it.

5. A COMPARISON OF MY LIFE BETWEEN ISLAM AND JESUS CHRIST

My Life with Islam	*My Life with Jesus Christ*
Islam didn't give me a guarantee of salvation from Hell-fire.	Jesus saved my from hell and gave me eternal life.
There was no love in my relationship with God, but fear from His punishment and love of His Paradise which is full of beautiful women and wine which He forbade us to use here on earth. This in addition to eating meat and fruit and being in bed, engaging in sex with seventy women every night.	My life with Jesus is based on love and friendship and not fear here on earth. In heaven, after death, a life in the presence of God in His heavenly Kingdom.
I didn't have peace in my heart and wasn't at peace with others.	My heart has been filled with peace and I have been living in peace with others.
I couldn't love everybody. I used to love some and hate others, whether they are Muslims or not.	Because Jesus loves the whole world and He came to die on the Cross for them, this taught me to love everybody and to pray for them.
I used to believe that Jihad is killing all enemies of Islam.	Now I believe that Jihad is against spiritual evil in order for me to do God's will.

My Life with Islam	*My Life with Jesus Christ*
I used to feel sorry for the Muslim woman whom Islam made into a possession for man. Her inheritance and her court witness is half of that of a man. The policy of exclusion and mistrust in her relationship with men. If a Muslim girl fell in love with a man, even if she didn't commit any wrong act, this would be enough reason to kill her. I can never forget my classmate Hassan who took a chopper and slaughtered his sister because he saw her walking with a friend whom she was in love with.	I found that the Bible gave the woman honour and made her equal with man in all rights and responsibilities. I found the relationship between man and woman based on trust, love and respect. This is great trust which the Christian girl enjoys and her understanding to everything around her, and this relationship in marriage with God made from the wife and the husband one flesh where there is no divorces or polygamy. In a few words, it is a life in the presence of God and separated from all the vanity of this world.
I was living in fear of death if it confronts me while I am not engaged in battle with the enemies of Islam. I thought that if I die in a natural way I will go through the dreadful experience when the angel of death comes to take my spirit starting from my toe nails, all the way to my mouth. This in addition to the fearful agony I have to face in the grave when the two angels will give an account about me and the grave will turn either to a garden of Paradise if I was found to be a good doer, or it can turn out to be a pit of fire if I am to be found an evil doer, and the snakes who are as big as mules will come and bite me.	Now I feel peace and comfort. I do not fear death at all, whether I die at the hands of nonbelievers or I die from natural causes. Death to me is like a plane or rocket which will carry me to my Lord and Saviour Jesus Christ, whom I love. It will be a happy union with the one I love, no tormenting in the grave, no snakes the size of mules, and no donkeys.

My Life with Islam	*My Life with Jesus Christ*
I was arrogant and liked to boast and work at glorifying my name and my family's name. I used to envy anybody who did better than I did at school or at work.	I became humble in front of the Lord. I came to look at myself as one who is not better than others. I became to feel that I am modest who needs God's hand. I live now to only glorify Jesus Christ. I don't envy anyone, but I love everyone.
I used to perform the rituals such as praying and fasting, etc., out of fear and to gain praises from others.	Now I obey the Lord and pray and fast because I love Him and find joy in doing that. I do this in secrecy so that nobody will see me and praise me for it.
I didn't know what the future will bring as far as the after death, whether I'll be going to Paradise or Hell-fire.	I know now where I am heading to after death, Heaven, there where I'll be in the company of the Lord Jesus Christ.

6. A COMPARISON BETWEEN JESUS CHRIST AND MOHAMMED

What the Bible Says	*What the Qur'an Says*
Jesus Christ is the Son of God *As for me, the Father chose me and sent me into the world. How then can you say that I blaspheme because I say that I am the Son of God?* Joh 10:36	Mohammed was mortal man *Say: "I am but a man like yourselves...* S 18:101
Jesus Christ performed miracles *And all who heard were completely amazed. "How well He does everything!" they exclaimed. "He even causes the deaf to hear and the dumb to speak."* Mark 7:37	Mohammed didn't perform miracles *And We refrain from sending the Signs, only because the men of former generations treated them as false...* S 17:59

What the Bible Says	***What the Qur'an Says***
Jesus knew what was in the heart of man *...and then all churches will know that I am the one who knows every one's thoughts and wishes...* Rev 2:23	Mohammed did not know what was in the heart of man *I tell you not that with me are the Treasures of Allah, nor do I know what is hidden...* S 11:31
Jesus Christ is our intercessor before the Father. He pleads with the Father on our behalf. *I am writing this to you, my children, so that you will not sin; but if anyone does sin, we have someone who pleads with the Father on our behalf - Jesus Christ* 1 Joh 2:1	Mohammed does not intercede for his people. *Whether thou ask for forgiveness, or not, (their sin is unforgivable): If thou ask seventy times for their forgiveness, Allah will not forgive them...* S 9:80
Jesus prohibited his followers from using violence or the sword. *"Put your sword back in his place," Jesus said to him. "All who take the sword will die by the sword."* Mat 26:52	Mohammed encouraged his followers to use the sword. *O Prophet! rouse the Believers to the fight, If there are twenty amongst you, patient and persevering, they will vanquish two hundred: if a hundred, they will vanquish a thousand of the Unbelievers: for these are a people without understanding.* S 8:65
Jesus preached forgiveness *"You have heard that it was said, 'An eye for an eye, and a tooth for a tooth.' But I now tell you: do not take revenge on someone who wrongs you. If anyone slaps you on the right cheek, let him slap you on the left cheek too.* Mat 5:38,39	Mohammed preached revenge *...There is the law of equality. If then any one transgresses the prohibition against you, transgress ye likewise against him...* S 2:194
Jesus Christ was without sin. (No sin was found in him.) *He committed no sin, and no one ever heard a lie come from his lips.* 1 Pet 2:22	Mohammed was a sinner. *Know, therefore, that there is no god but Allah, and ask forgiveness for thy fault, and for the men and women who believe...* S47:19

What the Bible Says	*What the Qur'an Says*
Jesus rebuked the Devil *Then Jesus answered, "Go away, Satan! The scripture says, 'Worship the Lord your God and serve only him!'"* Mat 4:10	Mohammed used to meet with spirits. *Behold, We turned towards a company of Jinn (quietly) listening to the Qur'an: when they stood in the presence thereof, they said, "Listen in silence!" When the (reading) was finished, they returned to their people, to warn them.* S 46:29
The Devil never had authority over Jesus. *I cannot talk with you much longer, because the ruler of this world is coming. He has no power over me...* Joh 14:30	Mohammed was under the authority of the Devil. *If a suggestion from Satan assail thy (mind), seek refuge with Allah;* S 7:200
Jesus healed the blind. *So Jesus stopped and ordered the blind man to be brought to Him. When he came near, Jesus asked him, "What do you want me to do for you?"* *"Sir, he answered, "I want to see again."* *Jesus said to him, "Then see! Your faith has made you well." At once he was able to see...* Luk 18:40-43	Mohammed turned his face away from the blind. *(The Prophet) frowned and turned away, because there came to him the blind man (interrupting).* S 80:1,2
Jesus called the people to come to Him *"Come to me, all of you who are tired of carrying heavy loads, and I will give you rest. Take my yoke and put it on you, and learn from me, because I am gentle and humble in spirit; and you will find rest. For the yoke I will give you is easy, and the load I will put on you is light."* Mat 11:28-30	Mohammed was rebuked by God when he sent the people away. *Send not away those who call on their Lord morning and evening, seeking His face. In naught art thou accountable for them, and in naught are they accountable for thee, that thou shouldst turn them away, and thus be (One) of the unjust...* S 6:52
Jesus blessed the marriage and preached monogamy. *"...And God said: 'For this reason a man will leave his father and mother and unite with his wife, and the two will become one.* Mat 19:5	Mohammed preached polygamy. *...Marry women of your choice, two, or three or four...* S 4:3

What the Bible Says	*What the Qur'an Says*
Jesus Christ came to save the world. *...for the Son of Man did not come to destroy men's lives, but to save them.* Luke 9:55	Mohammed preached war and fighting. *Say to the desert Arabs who lagged behind: "Ye shall be summoned (to fight) against a people given to vehement war: then shall ye fight, or they shall submit...* S 48:16
One has freedom to choose for or against Jesus *Listen! I stand at the door and knock; if anyone hears my voice and opens the door, I will come into his house and eat with him, and he will eat with me.* Rev 4:20	Mohammed forced people to accept Islam by the sword. *Fight those who believe not in Allah nor the Last Day, nor hold that forbidden which hath been forbidden by Allah and His Messenger, nor acknowledge the Religion of Truth, from among the People of the Book, until they pay the Jizya with willing submission, and feel themselves subdued.* S 9:29
Jesus is the Life. Those who believe in Him will be saved. *Jesus said to her, "I am the resurrection and the life. Whoever believes in me will live, even though he dies; and whoever lives and believes in me will never die..."* Joh 11:25	Mohammed is dead. His followers are unsure whether they will have eternal life or not. *Truly thou wilt die (one day), and truly they (too) will die (one day).* S 39:30

There is no comparison at all between the Lord Jesus Christ and any man, no matter how superior his is, because any man is still human but Jesus is Lord and God. The reason I made this comparison is just to give an illustration of the differences between the sinful man and the Lord and God who came to this world taking a form of a man and living among us, who was then crucified and died for all sinful human race.

7. WHAT THE QUR'AN SAYS ABOUT JESUS' CRUCIFICTION, DEATH AND RESURRECTION

In this section I will take you, my dear reader, to the Qur'an to show you what it said with regards to Jesus' death on the Cross and His ascension to heaven. When you see me quoting the Qur'an, I don't mean to prove the truthfulness of Jesus' death and ascension from the Qur'an. Not at all. I just wanted to draw attention to the contradictions in the Qur'an, which is one of its characteristics. No-one can find a single and straight line to its thoughts. However, the scholars of the Qur'an try to justify these contradictions under 'The abrogated and the abrogator' theory.

Let's see what the Qur'an has said about the death and ascension of Jesus. The Qur'an discussed this in two ways.
The first way, rejecting His crucifixion according to S4:157: *'-They slew him(Jesus) not nor crucified, but it appeared so unto them; and lo! those who disagree concerning it are in doubt thereof, they have no knowledge thereof save a pursuit of conjecture; they slew him not for certain, but Allah took him up unto Himself."*
This verse was mainly what I had believed in when I was a Muslim. I never had any doubt that Jesus never died or was crucified. Although I memorised the Qur'an since my childhood, I never gave any attention to other verses that can contradict this belief of Jesus as not having been crucified or killed.

But after returning from Iran and having seen Soura al-Wilaia, which doesn't exist in our Qur'an which belongs to the Sunni Sect, that Sura which is only accepted by the Shiits, made me go back to the Qur'an to study and analyse every single detail. I was surprised to discover the following: Four verses in three Suras talk about the death of Jesus and His ascension using three different verbs:

A. The Future Tense verb
   Allah uses this verb to pave the road to the killing of Christ in order to prepare their minds to receive this great event which will come in the future.*'Peace be on him(Jesus) the day he was born, and the day he (will) dieth and the day he shall be raised alive!" S19:15*

B. The Present Tense verb

Allah uses it to say: Pay attention, the death of Jesus will start within a short time.

'(And remember) when Allah said: O Jesus! Lo! I am gathering thee and causing thee to ascend unto Me, and am cleansing thee of those who disbelieve and am setting those who follow thee above thos who disbelieve until the Day of Resurrection." S3:55

When I looked at the verb 'Motawafik' (translated = will take thee) in the Islamic commentaries, I found Muslim scholars explain this as 'raising'. But when I started to analyse it linguistically, I discovered that there are two present tense verbs in this verse, each one having a definite meaning different from the other. The first 'Motawafik' and the second 'Rafaak'. The second verb explains the meaning of the first. The second means 'I will raise thee' which will confirm the meaning of the first to be 'I'll cause you to die.' It doesn't make sense to mention two verbs meaning the same thing, which is 'I will raise thee.'

C. The Past Tense Verb

The past tense in the Arabic language is used to mean that the event had already happened and is done with. In this sense, the Qur'an declares that the death of Jesus has already happened.

'I (Jesus) was a witness of them while I dwelt among them, and when Thou tookest(killed in Arabic) me wast the whatch over them..." S5:177

Here you find the verb 'Tawafitani', a past tense verb which means that the death had already happened.

You can now see my dear reader, how the Qur'an contradicted itself in regard to this serious subject. It never settles this matter and presented to the world one clear position to convince those who doubt it, not to mention those who follow it.

8. TWO MUSLIM FUNDAMENTALISTS CAME TO KILL ME

I did not tell anyone except the pharmacist and her husband that I gave my heart to Jesus, so little people knew that I was a Christian. There are many Muslim fundamentalist groups in Egypt functioning in schools and other organisations. These groups of people knew me very well since the days that I was still at school and university. They also knew me as Imam in Giza City and after I quit my work at the university and stopped working as an Imam, knew that I had left the Islamic religion.

In Egypt, if anyone left Islam, it is automatically assumed by everyone that he became a Christian. The fundamentalists also understood it like this and sent two men in Giza City to ambush me in Tersae street and kill me.

When I came to Tersae street, they came at me with knives and tried to stab me in my heart. Miraculously, they missed and hit me in my shoulder. I fell down with blood pouring from the gaping wound. I was curled into a little ball. The next man tried to stab me in my abdomen, but he turned the blade slightly and hit my shins on the left leg.

By this time many people had gathered around to see what was happening and yet nobody came to help me. They also didn't understand why these men wanted to kill me.

At that very moment, when I thought that there was no hope left for me, God send two traffic officers on motorcycles to pass through that street. Immediately, they stopped to see what the commotion was, and the two fundamentalists saw them and fled.

An ambulance arrived to take me to Om Al Masriien hospital. The police visited me in the hospital to enquire about this accident. I told them that I didn't know who these people was.

Jesus Christ protected me there, this proved that nobody could take away this new life that He gave me.

CHAPTER 5

FACE TO FACE WITH DEEDAT

1. MY FATHER SENT ME TO SOUTH AFRICA

In 1994 certain political changes took place in South Africa. For the first time, they also had a black ruler. New doors opened and the problems between South Africa and The Arab world had been resolved. After South Africa had opened an embassy in Cairo my father, being a business man, wanted to know what the business situation is like in South Africa and thus sent me to Johannesburg. I was to send any information gathered there to him by fax.

I arrived on the Fourth of August 1994 in Johannesburg and initially I was very impressed, only to be disillusioned later. I stayed in Johannesburg for 1 day and then left for Durban. I believed that since there was a large Muslim community in Durban, I could easily establish clothing materials business ties there.

We thought that because we are all Muslims, that they will welcome me as a Arab Muslim. I was however, surprised that as a matter of fact, they hated the Arab Muslims and despised them. Why is that? I don't really know.

2. FACE TO FACE WITH DEEDAT

Mr Deedat is an Indian Muslim from South Africa. He founded an Islamic Centre in the city of Durban with the support of the Gulf countries for the purpose of attracting Christianity and casting doubts on the Bible. He wrote twenty small booklets in which he attacked the Christian faith. This is in addition to may tracts he made to preach to Christians and to convert them to Islam. He also participated in may debates with Christians.

This man is not really knowledgeable in Islam, because he is not at all qualified for that. He doesn't speak Arabic, doesn't memorize the whole Qur'an, doesn't know anything from the Hadith. He never studied Islam in an Islamic university, thus he can't qualify to be an Islamic scholar. In addition to that, you will find many people in the Islamic world who consider him a scholar on the Bible, and this is a big lie that has deceived many Muslims. The truth is completely different. This man is not a Christian, and he doesn't know the original languages in which the Bible was written, the Hebrew, the Aramaic or the Greek. He only tried to study the Bible through the English translation which is not sufficient. He didn't study the history of the bible or God's people. He didn't study the bible's geography nor did he study the ancient civilizations of nations that dealt with God's people. He also didn't study theology in a specialised school.

After my arrival in Durban, I telephoned Mr Deedat and presented myself to him as a former teacher of history and Islamic civilization at al-Azhar University and that I am a businessman who came to South Africa. I asked him for a meeting. They gave me an appointment to see him at 10h00 on Friday at his office on the fourth floor in a big glass-faced building on Queen Street in downtown Durban.

When I met him, I was surprised to discover that he doesn't speak Arabic at all. He called on a man who could hardly speak Arabic to help me with the conversation.

We talked about different subjects related to Islam and Christianity, about the work of his centre and the financial support he receives from different Arab countries. He pointed to some photographs of princes from Saudi Arabia and Gulf countries hanging on his office wall. He explained to me how they love him and support him generously.

Before I left this man, I was certain that his knowledge of Islam doesn't exceed the knowledge of an elementary student at al-Azhar University by much.

As I was leaving, I asked him about the possibility of exchanging some American Dollars to South African currency. He told me that I don't need to go to the bank, that he can do that for me. He asked his brother Kassim Deedat to assist me. Kassim took me to his office where the safe of the centre is located. There he exchanged the Dollars for Rands.

I left the office of Mr Deedat after I knew everything about this man. I found out about the true Deedat, that he is only a businessman and not a scholar in either Islam or Christianity. This man also refused to help me find a bank, but rather did the exchange himself in his centre which is against the law in South Africa as it is harmful to the country's economy. Another thing is that he exchanged the Dollar for 3 Rands and 75 cents. This man then stole 750 Rands from me which is the difference between him and the bank for the amount of one thousand Dollars that he had exchanged.

My amazement stopped when I discovered that the man owned many stores in the commercial area around Queen Street in Durban.

How ugly it is to use faith as a tool for business and making money. A man like this doesn't mind making his money in order to gain money from the Gulf princes or from anybody else.

3. THREE DAYS WITH A CHRISTIAN FAMILY IN DURBAN

Initially, when I arrived in Durban I booked into a hotel, and stayed there for twelve days. I was content at that time because I saw that South Africa was a beautiful country. During this time I met an Indian Christian who was working at the hotel as a musician. He and his wife came to visit me in the hotel. It was the first time that they had met an Egyptian. They seemed to like me and asked whether I would rather stay with them in their house than in the hotel. I told them that I have only three days left in South Africa but that I would love to stay with them. During these three days I stayed in a lovely prepared room and they also made arrangements to take me on trips in Natal and also to some family members in Petermaritzburg. For the first time in my life I lived a Christian life - for three days I prayed before we ate, before going to bed, after waking up in the morning and I visited Church for the first time.

Those were some of the most beautiful days in my life, I will never forget these first Christian days of my life. This family played an important part in helping me to understand life as a Christian.

When the three days was over, they took me to the airport where we said goodbye. We all cried a little as the parting was a sad occasion and made arrangements to see each other again. The man gave me a beautiful golden cross pendant and said: *'Even if you forget us, do not forget Jesus Christ whom you have accepted as your Saviour who will give you every blessing in heaven and on earth.'*

I boarded the plane to Johannesburg after which I returned to Cairo with South African Airways.

4. MY FATHER REALISED THAT I HAD CONVERTED TO CHRISTIANITY

After 16 days in South Africa I was back in Cairo. I wore the cross around my neck on a chain for about ten days before my father

noticed the chain on my neck. He was upset because according Islamic culture only woman are allowed to wear jewellery around their necks.
My father asked me: *'Why do you wear this chain?'*
Upon looking back, I cannot say how I spoke for it seems that my tongue spoke by itself. There was power in me that I had never known before.

I answered him: *'Father, this is not a chain, this is a cross. This cross resembles Jesus, who died on a cross like this, for me, and for you, and for everybody in the whole world. I received Jesus Christ as my God and Saviour, and I pray for you and for the rest of my family to also accept Jesus Christ as your Saviour.'*

Upon hearing this my father's face went pale and he fainted. My brothers heard the cries of the women in the street who saw my father collapse and thought that he had died. They quickly rushed down to the street to carry him into the building. My mother was shocked and started crying while my brothers bathed my father's face with water to try and restore his consciousness.

When my father came round everybody wanted to know what had happened. He was so upset that he could hardly speak. His face was filled with tears as he cried out in a high pitched voice: *'Your brother is a convert! I must kill him today!'*
He reached for his gun, and pointed at me, I started running, and as I dived for cover I heard the bullets wining past me. I safely made it around a corner out of reach of the bullets and I kept running...

> When looking back on that day I think of what Jesus said: *'I know my sheep, and my sheep knows me, ...'*

Psalm 91

Whoever goes to the Lord for safety, whoever remains under the protection of the Almighty, can say to him, 'You are my defender and protector. You are my God; in you I trust.'
He will keep you safe from all dangers and from all deadly diseases. You need not fear any dangers at night or sudden attacks during the day or the plagues that strike in the dark or the evils that kill in daylight.
A thousand may fall dead beside you, ten thousand all around you, but you will not be harmed. You will look and see how the wicked are punished.
You have made the Lord your defender, the Most High your protector, and no disaster will strike you, no violence will come near your home.
God will put his angels in charge of you to protect you wherever you go. They will hold you up with their hands to keep you from hurting your feet on the stones. You will trample down lions and snakes, fierce lions and poisonous snakes.
God says, 'I will save those who love me and protect those who know me as Lord. When they call to me, I will answer them; when they are in trouble, I will be with them. I will rescue them and honour them. I will reward them with long life; I will save them.'

I ran to the house of my sister and at this time I realised that it is important for me to flee and leave Egypt. I asked my sister to help me by fetching my passport, clothes and other documents at my house. She wanted to know what was wrong and I told her that our father wanted to kill me. She wanted to know why, and I said: *'I don't know, you must ask Father.'*

My father, who had followed me to my sister's house arrived at that moment and banged on the door crying with tears streaming down his face: *'My daughter, please open the door!'* Hitting the door even harder he said: *'Your brother is a convert! He has left the Islamic faith. I must kill him now!'*

My sister opened the door and told my father: *'Father, please calm down. My brother is fine, he is not a convert, did you forget that he was the first in our family to memorise the Qur'an? Do not listen to what the people is saying. My brother is a Sheikh and an Imam and a teacher at Al Azhar.'*
My father replied: *'Nobody told me! He told me himself! I know that he is in your house. Where is he? Show him to me so that I can kill him and meet Allah with peace.'*
My sister said: *'Father, he is not here, I have not seen him today. Maybe he went to another place, why don't you go home and relax for a while. I will come over later, then we can talk as a family.'*

My father then returned home, weeping.

I told my sister that I must leave the Middle East immediately. She fetched my clothes, passport and other belongings from my home. My mother gave her four thousand Egyptian pounds (±$1200) and when my sister returned home she gave me an additional three thousand Egyptian pounds (±$900).

Before leaving the home of my sister, I prayed to Jesus for strength and protection for the journey. I told Him that I knew that this was the start of the journey, but I did not know where it would end. I said that I trusted Him for the rest of my life, and that wherever I went, I would witness about Him, Jesus Christ the Lord.

When I finished praying, the Holy Spirit told me in my heart that God is very pleased with this journey, and that I have His blessing. I then started the trip, from Cairo to Libya via Alexandria on the coastal road...

CHAPTER 6

FACE TO FACE WITH DEATH IN THE SAHARA DESERT

1. I LEFT EGYPT AND FOLLOWED JESUS CHRIST

On the evening of the twenty eighth of August 1994 I started a very long and difficult journey - the first Middle Eastern man to undertake such a journey.

My reason for taking this journey was Jesus Christ. He was also my companion and teacher. Through the next few pages, you, my brother or sister, can see how God lead me every single step of the way.

I left Cairo to Alexandria, and from there to Al Salowme the last city before leaving Egypt. After Al Salowme, I went to Tobrok in Libya, then to Bangazi, and on to Tripoli, the capital of Libya. By then, in the time of six days, I had driven four thousand kilometres. In Tripoli I went to the Chadian embassy in to apply for a travel visa through Chad to Cameroon.

It was refused the first time. They explained to me that the Chadian government was angry with the Egyptian people because they refused visas for Chadian people. I told the man at the embassy that the Chadian government do to the Egyptian government what they did to the Chadian government. Yet Jesus Christ said that if you need a shirt, I must give you mine. Also love your enemy. Do you love your enemy?

The one man asked: *'Jesus Christ?'*
'Yes,' I said, *'Jesus Christ.'*
He then asked *'Are you then Christian or Muslim?'*
I replied: *'My passport says Muslim, but my heart, my tongue and my mind says that I am Christian.'*
His face changed and he went into another room saying: *'No, this embassy cannot give you a visa.'*
He then took my passport and threatened to stamp it with the dreaded REFUSED sign.

I said to him: *'Good, God can make anything right.'*
I then left the office and went outside into the embassy garden. I knelt under a large tree and started to pray. I read Psalms 53 and 91 and asked God to help me in this time. When I finished praying, I saw a Chadian girl from the offices coming to me and saying: *'Are you the Egyptian man?'*
I said *'Yes I'm him.'*
Then she said: *'You can come and take your visa. But tell me what did you do when you went out of the office?'*
'Nothing,' I said, *'I only spoke to my God and complained to Him for the way I am treated. He told me: Do not worry or be sad, I will give you everything you need. (Ps 75:3)''*
'Can you speak to God?' She exclaimed, *'Can any person be with God - and complain to Him?'*
'Yes,' I said, *'Christian people can speak to God.'*
I continued: *'Please give me a few minutes to give thanks to God.'*
I was very happy and read Psalm 104:33-35:

> *'I will sing to the Lord all my life;*
> *as long as I live I will sing praises to my God.*
> *May he be pleased with my song*
> *for my gladness comes from him.*
> *May sinners be destroyed from the earth;*
> *may the wicked be no more.*
> *Praise the Lord, my soul!*
> *Praise the Lord!'*

She said: *'I saw on your passport that you were a Muslim, but are you now a Christian?'*
'Yes, and I gave Him my life. I left Egypt to start this trip through Africa and everywhere I come I will tell the people about Jesus Christ.'
When I said this I saw tears in her eyes. And after a short silence she said: *I can see that you can talk to the Almighty God. You can complain to Him, praise Him, and thank Him, and He listens to you, I can see that and He has helped you. Please stay for a few days in Tripoli and teach me to talk to this God, to pray to Him and to talk to*

Him. From now on I will open my heart to Him. I want to understand how to live with Him.'
I asked her whether she was a Muslim, the answer was: *'Yes, I am from a Muslim family from north-east Chad.'*
At that moment I was so very happy I cried out: *'Praise the Almighty God! He allowed the people in this office to create a small problem in order for Him to save this girl.'*
I went to the office and took my passport and transit visa which was valid for 15 days. After I have left, I received a phone call from a man at this office who asked me to wait a few days and tell him how I accepted Jesus Christ as my Saviour. I inquired whether he is Muslim or Christian. He said that he is the only Christian in that embassy. He said that he was from Sarh City in South Chad. He continued by saying that when he heard about my problem at their office, he sat down with his Bible and prayed that God must make a miracle happen for me on that day. I told him that God has heard his prayer and that the visa is now in my passport and that God has saved the Muslim girl at that embassy. He promised me to teach her and help her with things about the Bible.

The next day I went to the embassy and met this man and the girl and told them my testimony. Before I left I asked them to pray with me for my difficult trip through Africa.

That day I left Tripoli and went to Kofrah, last city in South Libya. This city was the door to the Sahara Desert from Libya.

2. FACE TO FACE WITH DEATH IN THE SAHARA DESERT

After travelling for two and a half days covering 2200 kilometres, I arrived at Kofrah, a small city with few people. All the people in Kofrah are from Sudanese, Chadian and Lebanese backgrounds. I went to a travel agency and asked whether there were any vehicles leaving for Chad through the Sahara desert, but I was told that there is no road through the Sahara and also no vehicles that travel through the desert. Upon hearing this I was disheartened and asked the man what I was to do. He then told me that there were some people who crossed the desert by vehicle. They were black market traders, smuggling goods across the Chadian border and they used Land Cruisers stolen from the Libyan army. They also were willing to take passengers along and many Chadian people working in Libya used this as transport to Chad.

I asked where I could make contact with these people and a driver from the transport agency said that he knew a man who undertook these illegal trips, and that he would take me to his house.

When we arrived at this house it appeared, even from the outside, to be quite a shack. When I met the woman who owned the house many other things came as a shock to me. The woman was from a Chadian background, but now possessed Libyan citizenship. She also made a living by keeping prostitutes in her little house and running an escort agency. On top of all she was also selling liquor and drugs illegally.

The woman agreed to take me on this trip but wanted to know how much I would be paying. I replied that I have not taken such a trip before and that I did not know the price. She said that she would take me for $100 but I begged her to help me because my journey was long and my money very little. She finally agreed to take me for $50 but said that I will be dropped of at the very first Chadian city they reached.
I wanted to know how long the trip would be, She replied that it would take about 15 days. She told me to go to a hotel and wait, and warned me that I must be prepared to wait at least two weeks before her driver will pick me up with the jeep. Furthermore she said that I must buy supplies for the trip. I inquired as to what the supplies must be and she replied that I must buy two containers that can hold 25 litres of water each, 20 kilograms of onions and 25 kilograms of dates. That was all I needed for the trip she said. I wanted to know how I would be able to

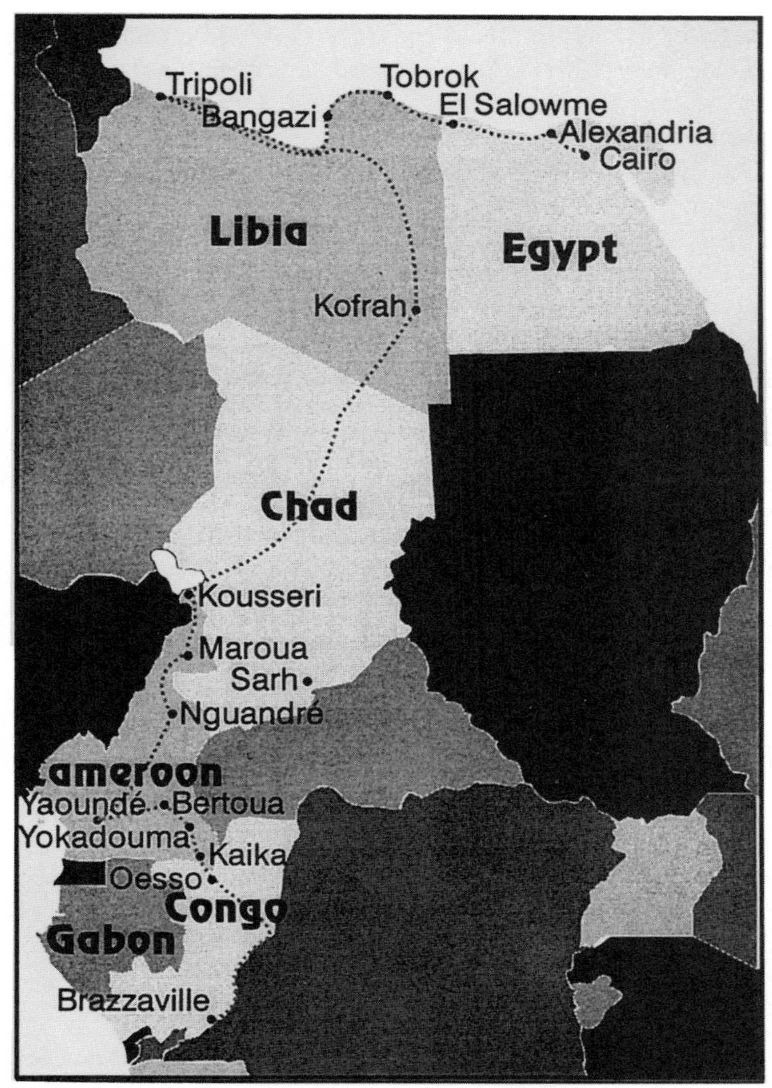

My route through Africa

survive for 15 days in the desert without meat or vegetables, but she said that in the Sahara you do not need these things. I also asked why then, must I take the onion - how would I be able to eat it? She replied that one is forced to eat onions in the Sahara, first of all to provide you with the necessary water and secondly to protect you from sunstroke. I said that I would rather buy fruit but she warned me that fruit would only make me more thirsty and I would only have the two containers of water.
'You are a child of the city,' she said, *'I am a child of the Sahara. Do what I say because I know what I am talking about.'*
I then agreed to do as she said.

I went to a hotel and waited 25 days before the driver with the Landcruiser came to pick me up, and we started our journey. There were 20 other young people from Chad also undertaking this journey, excluding the driver and a navigator. The Landcruiser were stacked on the back with flour and sugar and other sacks with trading goods and on top of this, the passengers were to sit. Our water containers were fastened to the sides and back of the Landcruiser, only the nose of the vehicle was clear.

It was as if the Landcruiser was waging war against the sand, stone, mountains and valleys. We were on a gigantic sea of sand and I didn't know how we would be able to find way through this dessert. Once we stopped and I saw the driver and navigator arguing. The driver took some sand and threw it in the air to check the direction of the wind. By this he knew which direction to travel. At night though, whenever there was an argument, they stopped to check the stars, and navigated by them.

The first morning when we stopped for breakfast, I took my portion of dates and onions and some water and walked some 50 metres away from the car to urinate after which I started to wash my face with some of the water. I was unaware that the driver was watching me. Suddenly I saw him running towards me, grabbing the water from my hands and hitting me in my face. *'What are you doing?'* he shouted.

I was shocked for I did not know what I had done wrong. I asked him why he hit me and he said: *'This water is not for washing, only for drinking. In the next few days you will see how important this water is for your survival. You are like someone who wants to kill himself!'*
I understood what he was saying but I told him that my eyes are very sore from all the dust. He took a little piece of cloth and dabbed it in a little water showing me to clean only my eyes with the piece of cloth. *'In future'*, he said *'once a day, you can clean your eyes like this.'*
'Thank you,' I said *'this was my very first lesson in the Sahara Desert.'*

Fifteen days into the desert, we had travelled 2000 km. We reached a place called 'Mount of the Forties' (also known as the ring of death.) We still had 1000 km to go but by this time, our water supply was finished. For three days we kept going, searching and hoping, but after the third day we were too exhausted to continue. When I got out of the vehicle I just fell into the sand, I couldn't move.

It seemed that death was eminent to all of us. I lay in the sand waiting to die when suddenly I found myself rising to my knees. I started praying: *'Oh God, you alone can help me. My Lord Jesus Christ, I know you said: "My sheep will follow me and I know my sheep." I am one of your flock, I am in your hands, exiled from my home, emigrating to you, seeking a place to worship you in freedom. I have no food, no water and death approaches. Please Lord, give me water to turn death away from me.'*
Suddenly a voice said to me: *'Go to the driver and tell him to leave this place immediately. Do not stay here any longer.'*

I rose and with the little strength I had left, I ran to the driver, saying: *'Can we take the car and leave this place?'*

'Are you crazy?' Was the reply, *'Here is like there, it's all the same and as you can see, we have fallen into the trap of the desert. There's no water here, there's no water there, we still have 1000 kilometres to go!'*
'I swear,' I cried. *'God said we will find water!'*
Finally he agreed and we all struggled back onto the Landcruiser.

After about ten minutes drive, I saw a small oasis in the distance.
I shouted: *'Look, water.'*
They laughed at me, *'It's only a mirage! We see it all the time. Why don't you stop hallucinating.'*
But as we got closer we all realised that indeed, it was not a mirage, it was a miracle from God. I must confess, I have never tasted water like that in all my life. We drank and jumped into it, we refilled our containers with enough to last us for the remainder of the journey. I sat down, tears steaming down my face. I felt that God loved me more than anyone else in the world. I prayed: *'Lord, I know that many people believe in you with their hearts and minds but I believe in you with my heart, my mind and my eyes!'*

We continued our journey till we reached the first district of Chad. Here our driver relayed the story to the police. They were astonished and told us that this area of the Sahara was known as the most dangerous part of the desert because of its lack of water.

3. DANGER IN CAMEROON

I received a visa to enter Cameroon. After two days I headed for Koussri. On arrival, I tried to find a vehicle to take me to the capital, Yaoundé. Unable to succeed, I could do nothing else than to travel to Maroua, in the North of Cameroon. Yet this would take us through 52 km known as the most dangerous part of Cameroon. We had to travel in a group, escorted by the defence force. We arrived very late that night in Maroua. The next morning, I departed for Ngaundéré where I met an Egyptian doctor. I stayed with him for three days before I left for Yaoundé.

4. CANNIBALS!

When I arrived at Yaoundé I went directly to the Congo embassy to apply for a visa to go into the Congo. After this I went to a transport agency because I wanted to leave for Bertoua City in South Cameroon. Upon inquiring about passage, I was told that since it had rained constantly for a few days, the dirt roads were unusable and that none of their vehicles would travel to Bertoua. I told them that I was a foreigner in Cameroon and asked how I could travel to Bertoua. They replied that I may be able to use the train.

I went to the station and took the train to Bertoua. Arriving there I met a Sudanese man who owned a restaurant. He invited me to stay for the night as his house and also asked me whether I am on this trip to look for work. He offered me a job at his restaurant but I declined and told him that this journey is not to find work.

Early the next morning the friendly man took me to a transport agency where I departed for Yokadouma in South Cameroon on a very old Volkswagen Microbus. The little vehicle was stacked with 21 passengers inside and 10 travelling on the roof of this old vehicle. After spending a night in Yokadouma, I left by car for the city of Kaika, the last city in Cameroon.

We arrived very late in the night and the next morning I inquired about crossing the Congo river to cross the border into the Congo. I was told that there are people travelling across in small boats. I had to board a boat in Kaika and the travel south east to the Congo, because straight opposite Kaika lived cannibal people to the eastern side of Gabon on the banks of the river, so I was forced not to travel through Gabon or East Congo. When we came to the place where the boat was to depart, I was quite amazed by our so-called boat! It was nothing more than a large tree trunk that was hollowed out with a single outboard motor at the back. There was space for about ten people sitting in a row on this boat and it was fully laden for this trip.

The people on the boat were all from Congo, Mauritian, Cameroonian and Singanian backgrounds.

We were about two hours away when suddenly our little canoe-boat tipped slightly to the side and we heard a Mauritian man shout. He jumped overboard and someone announced that the man's little boy fell overboard. The man searched frantically in the water but the current was too strong and he was unable to find the boy. After searching for quite a while the driver took us to the opposite shore from where we had started from and which was now quite close. He thought it best because we were all badly shocked and the trip back to Kaika where the only police station was, would take more than two hours.

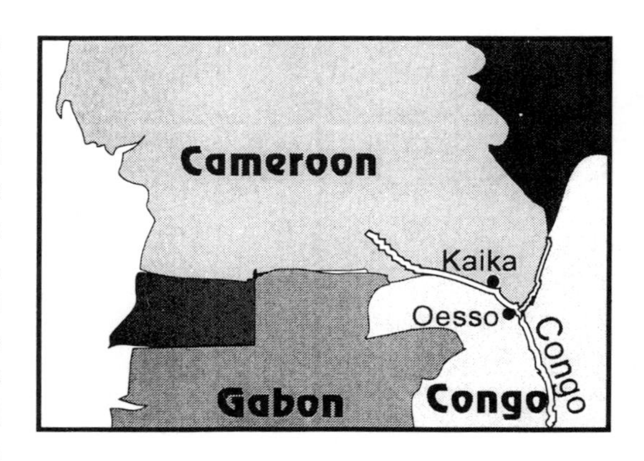

We were standing on the shore when suddenly a crowd of people burst out of the thick bush. Storming down on us, they suddenly froze in their tracks, turned around and started running back when our driver produced a gun and shot at them. I thought that they were only other Cameroonian people but the driver and other passengers told me that they were cannibals.

After this scary ordeal we comforted the poor Mauritian man and he agreed to continue down to Oesso and ask the police there to search for his son.

Arriving at Oesso I went to the police station to have my passport stamped, but the man took my passport and said that I would have to stay in the police station for a week or maybe ten days. I inquired as to the reason for this he answered that the only road which led to Brazzaville was a dirt road which had almost been washed away from the rain. Brazzaville was 1200 kilometres away. There weren't any vehicles leaving for Brazzaville and only in a week's time would there be transport again.

I waited for ten days before I boarded a car that left for Brazzaville but after only 150 kilometres, the engine broke down. Before the driver left the car to attend to the problem, he closed all the windows and told us to lock the doors. He explained that there were cannibals staying in those parts.

The driver had barely left the vehicle when people came running from the trees and bushes. The driver was prepared though and fired a few shots at them and since they do not have any weapons themselves and were scared, they ran back into the bush.

When the driver completed the work on the engine, we resumed our journey and finally arrived safely in Brazzaville.

5. A DOCTOR IN BRAZZAVILLE ASKED ME WHETHER I AM A MAN LIKE HIM, OR PERHAPS SOMETHING ELSE...

It was three months since I have left Egypt. I had seen different kinds of climates: Middle Sea, Sahara, Central Africa and West Africa. My body was very weak and I was tired. I had vaccinations before I left Libya to protect me from African diseases. Yet even that didn't prevent me from getting malaria three days before arriving in Brazzaville.

When I finally reached the city I was very weakened. I didn't walk far in the city before I fainted in a street. Someone robbed me of some of my clothes and my money, leaving only my passport and university degree certificates. I was still unconscious when policemen took me to a military hospital where I was admitted to the intensive care unit. I was unconscious when some drips were placed in my arm but the doctors told the hospital management that it was just a question of time before I would be dead. The hospital management contacted the Egyptian embassy in Brazzaville telling them that I was fatally ill and to request for a coffin to send my body back to Cairo. The embassy contacted the Consulate who came to visit me in the hospital. The Consulate sent for an Egyptian doctor in the Congo to examine me. The Egyptian doctor stayed by my bed till late that night to see if there was any recovery and when he finally left he telephoned the Consulate telling him that before the next morning, I will be dead. The doctor left and went to bed.

The next morning the coffin sent by the embassy arrived at the hospital, but I awoke as anyone would after having a peaceful night's rest. I sat up in my bed and said the only French word I knew to the other patients in the room: *'Bonjour'*

They were so shocked to see my miraculous recovery that they couldn't say a word. A nurse working the morning shift knew that my coffin had arrived earlier that morning. She was told that I wouldn't make it through the night, but when she walked into the room and saw me sitting upright on my bed, praying, she simply fainted. The other patients in my room called for help and many people came to see what had happened and some of them took the nurse away. The Egyptian doctor came rushing into the room and when he saw me he approached me carefully saying: *'Are you a man like me?'*

'Yes doctor,' I replied, *'I am a man.'*

'How then,' he asked, *'did you wake up this morning? Why are you sitting in this bed? When every test that we did, blood and urine specimens showed that you should have been dead by now?'*

'I can tell you why I am alive.' I said.

He urged me to do so.

'I left Egypt three months ago to follow my God,' I said, *'Jesus Christ. Jesus said in the Bible:*

The danger of death was round me,

and the grave sat it's trap for me.
In my trouble I called to the Lord;
I called to my God for help:
In his temple he heard my voice;
he listened to my cry for help''
(Psalm 18:5-7)

The man said: *'How can you know Jesus Christ? You passport states that you are a Muslim. You have taught at Al Azhar.'*
'Not Al Azhar,' I replied, *'nor my passport could prevent Jesus Christ from coming into my life giving me eternal life and saving me specially from all my sins.'*
He said: *'No power in the world can stop Jesus Christ from coming into your life if He wants to. I am a Christian, but this is the first time in my life that I have seen this. Today you have given me a sweet reminder of what Jesus Christ's name can do.'*
'Why do you tell me all these things,' He asked, *'even though you do not know whether I am a Muslim or a Christian?'*
I said: *'I don't know. I said these words even in Egypt before I came here and I do not know how I did it then. Perhaps it was the Holy Spirit who spoke these word through me.'*

I left the hospital after five days and started to tell the people everywhere about what Jesus did for me in Africa.

Now I am travelling the world, telling my story, this is the truth, please listen to me...

MY CRY

There is nothing left for me other than to cry out to all Muslims and other Non-Christians - to all humanity.

Come, all of you who are lost in the Sahara of deceitfulness. Rejoice you orphans, for the Lord Jesus is calling you and saying: 'I am the bread of life, come to me.' He will accept you with all your sin. Here, encircled in the arms of Jesus, our bodies are cleansed. Our hearts are purified, consciences and souls are relieved. To all sinners in the world who know that all types of humanity hate you, the Lord accepts you because He loves you. So you will be born again and forget that you were once sinners. All darkness will fade before your eyes displaced by the light of a new dawn - the one sparse moment in your life to rush forward with the believers in Jesus Christ the Saviour!

Jeremiah 29:13: '*You will seek me, and you will find me because you seek me with all your heart.*'

THE END